The All About Series
All About ... Canadian Attractions

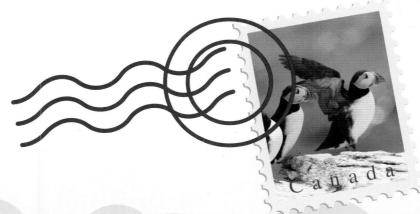

Canada

Cape Breton Highlands
National Park

Barb McDermott and Gail McKeown
Reidmore Books

Reidmore Books Inc.

18228 - 102 Avenue
Edmonton, AB T5S 1S7
phone (780) 444-0912
toll-free 1-800-661-2859
fax (780) 444-0933

website: http://www.reidmore.com
email: reidmore@compusmart.ab.ca

printed and bound in Canada

We acknowledge the financial support of the
Government of Canada through the
Book Publishing Industry Development Program (BPIDP)
for our publishing activities.

Canada

©1999 Reidmore Books

Canadian Cataloguing in Publication Data
McDermott, Barb.
All about Canadian attractions : Cape Breton Highlands National Park

(All about series)
Includes index.
ISBN 1-896132-41-3

1. Cape Breton Highlands National Park (N.S.)—Juvenile literature.
I. McKeown, Gail. II. Title. III. Series: McDermott, Barb. All about series.
FC2314.C36M32 1999 j971.6'91 C99-910583-3 F1039.C16M32 1999

About the Authors

Barb McDermott and Gail McKeown are highly experienced
kindergarten teachers living in Ontario. Both hold Bachelor of Arts and
Bachelor of Education degrees, Early Childhood diplomas, specialist
certificates in Primary Education, and have completed qualification
courses in Special Education. As well, Gail has a specialist certificate in
Reading and Visual Arts, and Barb has one in Guidance.

Credits

Editorial: Leah-Ann Lymer, Scott Woodley, David Strand,
Debbie Culbertson, Alice Blokland
Illustration, design and layout: Bruno Enderlin, Leslieanna Blackner Au
Maps: Wendy Johnson, Johnson Cartographics

Photo Credits

Table of Contents

(All about what's in the book)

Introduction
(All about the beginning)

Cape Breton **Highlands** National Park is a 95 000 hectare park with a **plateau** and rocky **coast**.

The park is located in the **province** of Nova Scotia.

The 1st people to live in the park area were the Mi'kmaq.

The park was created in 1936.

The park was made to **protect** the land, water, animals, and plants.

Cape Breton Highlands National Park

1

Location
(All about where Cape Breton Highlands National Park is in Canada)

Cape Breton Highlands National Park is located in northern Nova Scotia.

The park is located on Cape Breton **Island.**

The park is located in the Appalachian Highland.

The park is located beside the Gulf of St. Lawrence and the Cabot Strait.

Gulf of
St. Lawrence

Cabot Strait

PRINCE EDWARD
ISLAND

**Cape Breton Highlands
National Park**

Cabot
Trail

Ingonish Beach

NEW
BRUNSWICK

Cape Breton
Island

N

W · E

S

NOVA
SCOTIA

ATLANTIC
OCEAN

ARCTIC
OCEAN

YUKON

NORTHWEST
TERRITORIES

NUNAVUT

PACIFIC
OCEAN

BRITISH
COLUMBIA

ALBERTA

SASKATCHEWAN

MANITOBA

Hudson
Bay

ATLANTIC
OCEAN

NEWFOUNDLAND

ONTARIO

QUEBEC

PRINCE EDWARD
ISLAND

NOVA
SCOTIA

NEW
BRUNSWICK

History
(All about how Cape Breton Highlands
National Park began)

The land in Cape Breton Highlands National Park was
created 1 000 000s of years ago.

The land has been covered by **glaciers.**

Many groups of people have had **settlements** in the park area.

The park has a hut that looks like the home of a settler from
long ago.

Cape Breton Highlands was the 1st national park in the
Atlantic provinces.

A Settler's Hut

5

Land
(All about the land in Cape Breton Highlands National Park)

Cape Breton Highlands National Park has the highland plateau.

The highland plateau covers most of the park.

The highland plateau has hills, **valleys,** and **canyons.**

Cape Breton Highlands has a rocky coast.

Cape Breton Highlands Has a Rocky Coast

Land
(All about the land in Cape Breton Highlands National Park)

Cape Breton Highlands National Park has the highest land in Nova Scotia.

The highest land in the park is White Hill.

White Hill is 532 m tall.

The most rugged, rocky land in Nova Scotia is found in the park.

Cape Breton Highlands Has Rocky Land

Waterways
(All about the water in Cape Breton Highlands National Park)

Cape Breton Highlands National Park has many rivers including the Cheticamp, MacKenzie, and Grande Anse.

Many rivers in the park have **tannic acid.**

The park has many waterfalls including the Mary Ann and Beulach Ban falls.

The park also has lakes and **bogs.**

Cape Breton Highlands Has Rivers

Vegetation
(All about the plants in Cape Breton Highlands National Park)

Cape Breton Highlands National Park has an acadian land region.

This acadian land region is located in the lower parts of valleys.

Trees with leaves and some trees with needles grow in the acadian land region.

The acadian land region has trees that can live for more than 300 years!

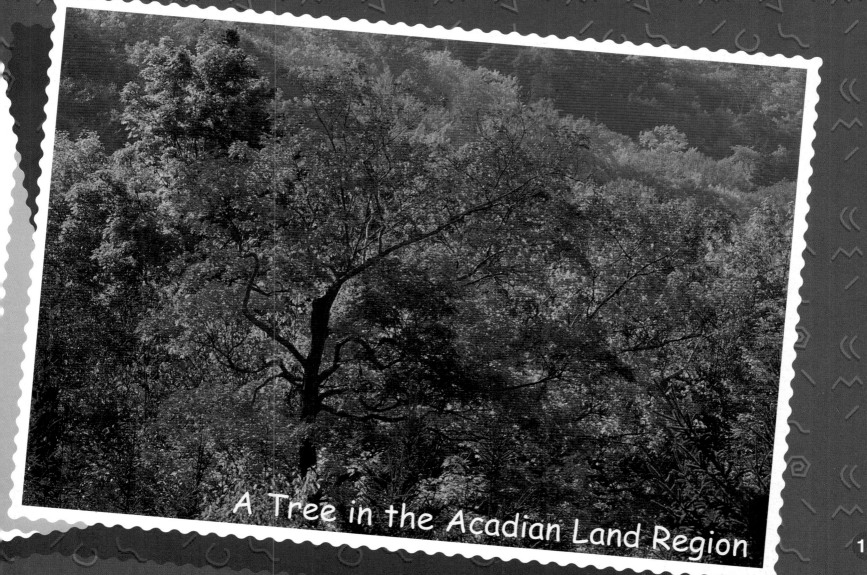

A Tree in the Acadian Land Region

13

Vegetation
(All about the plants in Cape Breton Highlands National Park)

Cape Breton Highlands National Park has a boreal and a taiga land region.

This boreal land region is located in the higher parts of valleys and on low hills.

The boreal land region has trees with needles.

The taiga land region is located on high plateaus.

The taiga land region has **lichens** and trees with needles.

There Are 2 Kinds of Trees in This Forest

Wildlife
(All about the animals in Cape Breton Highlands National Park)

Cape Breton Highlands National Park has many animals including whitetailed deer, red foxes, and black bears.

Cape Breton Highlands National Park is 1 of 4 parks in the world that protect Atlantic salmon.

Pilot, fin back, and minke whales live in and near the park.

A Whitetailed Deer

Wildlife
(All about the animals in Cape Breton Highlands National Park)

Cape Breton Highlands National Park has many kinds of birds.

Arctic terns, herring gulls, great cormorants, and Atlantic puffins live near the park's coast.

The park has red-tailed hawks, great horned owls, hermit thrushes, chickadees, gray jays, woodpeckers, bald eagles, and spruce grouse.

The park protects most of Nova Scotia's bald eagles.

Cape Breton Highlands Has Puffins

Places to Visit
(All about what to see in Cape Breton Highlands National Park)

Cape Breton Highlands National Park has Cabot Trail.

Cabot Trail is a famous highway that goes beside the park's beautiful, rocky coast.

Cabot Trail is 300 km long.

Cabot Trail was named after the **explorer** John Cabot.

Cabot Trail Is Beautiful

Places to Visit
(All about what to see in Cape Breton Highlands National Park)

Cape Breton Highlands National Park has the Keltic Lodge.

The Keltic Lodge was built in 1940.

The Keltic Lodge is located near Ingonish Beach.

Golfers love to visit the Keltic Lodge.

The Keltic Lodge is located near 1 of the best golf courses in Canada.

The Keltic Lodge

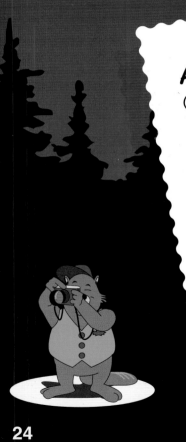

Activities
(All about what to do in Cape Breton Highlands National Park)

Cape Breton Highlands National Park has Ingonish Beach.

Ingonish Beach is sandy and is beside an ocean and a lake.

People can watch birds and whales in the park.

Cape Breton Highlands has ski hills and 26 hiking trails.

People can also camp, ride bikes, or swim in the park.

Ingonish Beach

Summary
(All about the ending)

Cape Breton Highlands National Park has a plateau, valleys, White Hill, a rocky coast, rivers, and Cabot Trail.

People come to the park to hike, ski, ride bikes, swim, and watch wildlife.

The park is located beside the Gulf of St. Lawrence and the Cabot Strait.

Cape Breton Highlands National Park is an amazing attraction ... found in Canada!

Cape Breton Highlands Has Valleys

Glossary
(All about what the words mean)

Atlantic (page 4)
Atlantic means near the Atlantic Ocean. The Atlantic provinces are New Brunswick, Nova Scotia, Prince Edward Island, and Newfoundland.

bogs (page 10)
Bogs are areas of soft, wet land.

canyons (page 6)
Canyons are narrow valleys with high, steep sides.

coast (page 1)
A coast is land along the edge of an ocean.

explorer (page 20)
An explorer is someone who goes into unknown areas.

glaciers (page 4)
Glaciers are large sheets of ice. Glaciers move slowly and push dirt and rocks.

highlands (page 1)
Highlands are an area of land that is raised.

island (page 2)
An island is a piece of land surrounded by water.

lichens (page 14)
Lichens are flowerless plants that grow on rocks and trees. Lichens are grey, yellow, brown, black, or green.

plateau (page 1)
A plateau is an area of land that is raised.

protect (page 1)
To protect something is to defend it from harm.

province (page 1)
A province is a separate region in Canada that has its own government.

settlements (page 4)
A settlement is a group of people living in the same place.

tannic acid (page 10)
Tannic acid is a brown-coloured acid that comes from some kinds of plants. Tannic acid can come from plants in bogs. There is tannic acid in tea.

valleys (page 6)
A valley is land between hills or mountains.